ARTIO

Julia Lally

DEDICATION

To the city of Bern, and all the witches who live in her.

TABLE OF CONTENTS

ACKNOWLEDGMENTS

With love to my husband Sean and son Oak who accompany me in all my artistic temperaments and personal follies.

Pagan Prayer

Life will tear at your chest
Rip from stomach to throat
A tender pink strip of flesh
Put it back
Gently tap it in
And smooth down the edges like
Wet clay
Hard, wet granite of pagan past
Let us take from you your solid spirit
Grey, determined
It is from our open, lotus-flesh wounds
That we must rise and gain reluctant force.

1994 - Boulder, Colorado, US

Devon Springtime

Relief throws open windows
After these long, coughing months
Of colds and limits
And nothing to view
Just the suffocating
Threat of
Winter's mildew
Weeks of it too,
Months of it
Until the clouds
In their sympathy
Began letting the long light through.

1995 - Totnes, Devon UK

America

This is not my land.

I wanted to expand…..
Feel myself opening
To vast currents of air

Be carried on riptides
Like your
Golden Eagle…
But instead

I have been badly beaten
By natural turbulence
As the land here is
Scarlet with
Sheer rage.

Listen to the earth
Like a brave.

The wilderness is growing
The coming storm is sucking in
Momentum and the
Clouds are gathering thunder.

Can you feel it?
Can you feel it?

It won't be long.

1994 – Boulder, Colorado, US

Mistaken Identity

I would rather strangle
On the umbilical chord
Of my own purple dissent
Pump up my veins in
Wretched discontent
Than shrink wrap my
Breathing organs to
Pulse alone in your accent
For it seems that
Each time you enter
I marshmallow myself together
And each time you go
I experience the low
The sickly static of
Sugar's afterglow
Oh either way I am lost
Like a glass-eyed fish
Who mouths it's silent misery
I swim in the world of you
I do.

1997 – Totnes, Devon, UK

One February Night in Washbourne

I remember
The night we all drank
Heady berry wine
And gusto-walked
To the top of
The green-furred hill.

Cold cold mud
To bare feet
Ice moon
Sending down silence
This February
Naked night.

Clothes came off
In warm skin layers
Retaining heat
In devotion
To our returning.

Wordlessly now,
Wearing another skin
We slipped in together
And ran
Strong and noiseless
Grouped across the hillside.

White limbs gleaming
Galloping in unison
This small, moonlight herd
Following it's instinct Westward.

1995 – Washbourne, Devon UK

Chemistry

I would like you to
Play with me,
Roll me
Between your palms,
Make me sing
Beloved,
I am a feast on a plate
It could be you, it could be me
Don't fill the space with
Metaphors
Be specific…
Sit with me,
Watch the fireworks
Crack in the hearth,
In this rough mix of
What you bring
Dressed in knowing
And what I bring
Cloaked in longing
Like colours
Like chemistry
Throwing hangovers to the wind
It is plain to see,
You are in my house now,
Whatever the weather
Making me sing
With this chime inside me
So soft you need to search for it,
And this sense of history
Both made and in the making.

2013 - Islington, London, UK

Switzerland

Tall trees
Far from home
Dry leaves
Dry as a bone
Frosted edges
Bright light
Blue sky
Deep night.

2022, Bern, Switzerland

The Black Hills

With changes that rip
And spin you to daze
So the natives
Spilling bloodshed
Were moved to barren lands
Of reservation and whiskey tears.

Still the high wind whispers angry to me –
For it is my kind
Buys dreamcatchers
That hang sad feathers in showrooms
My race stays at motels
Named after your ancient chief
My people buys sage sticks and
Novels on your struggle
From lilac painted bookstores.

No consolation then
That I may speak your cause
As it's me who roams
Over rocks sprouting crystals
And the aspens flap me greetings
In the land you know to be yours.

1994 - The Black Hills, South Dakota, US

Coffeeshop in Boulder

Dark nut wood
Shined to satin
Earthed with tweed
And the warmth of bricks
It's breathing texture
Steadies my pulse.

In accord the clock
Slows it's chested knock
Polite reminder
That time is eternal
And transcends even this.

Wind down now
Gulps of burnt brown
Bitter silk
Comfort
Like men
Who caress their
Tired old stubble and
The fragile pages of yellowed novels.

I yawn to exhale
Rising blue mist
Of cigarette's release
Flippant dismissal
Discarded ash
And surrender my flesh
To the slow steam outbreath
Of worlds where passions
Mellow to nonchalance.

1994 - Boulder, Colorado, US

Traditional Marriage

To change the mood
She paints her fingernails red
And tries to arrange the furniture
But it's still there
Echoing distantly in her head
Provide for me darling
And I will weep for you
She had said
Slipping on a ring
That was golden in it's promise
But gave her only
Power in the realm of the kitchen
Eventual boredom in her husband's bed
And the compromise of allowing
The flood of her heartbeat
To be determined by the
Direction of another instead.

1994 – Totnes, Devon UK

Crossing the Euston Road

Like an earthquake
On a line
Linear
And rumbling

The relentless noise
All the night and all the day
Even the autumn is rasping
That you notice
How she's silenced
How she's sad.

Sharp city in-breath and
I am stiff
Like the birds dancing high
Above St Pancras
Mad and restless
Twitchy
For the long haul.
It pulls at them now
The future.

Then the
Green man
The
Red man
The
Green man
Quick as death.

Home is calling me.
Home to him
Over this dangerous crossing
And the slippery, defeated leaves.

2013 - Kings Cross, London, UK

Time of the Month

There is a darkness
That trickles a tiny river
Inconspicuous and
Slow with the patience
Of centuries been bled.

You can see it in my pupils
If you look close enough
You can tell by
The way I suck fat
Off potato chips
And cut you dead
Hard as onyx.

For this is my time.
My Time.

1994 – Totnes, Devon, UK

Invitation on Beltane

My body is filling with wine
It is glowing through me
Accumulating age
It is brimming to my fingertips
Where I urge you to
Dive in with your golden roughness
And savour this ruby red fountain
Until the two of us are dribbling
And giggling with pleasure
And I am wearing white
And I feel like a cloud
And you show me your sword
And you boast
Bronze cuts to blood you say
But I am not deterred my love
As the juices always run this way
Forging history with mystery
Working the slippery ropes of tenderness
Until I am arching
I am muscular
And I invite you
Cup your hands and drink from me.

1994 – Totnes, Devon, UK

Sunrise

This is not a rude awakening
For the sun has singled me out!
I am cocooned like a chrysalis
Swathed in light
Fibrous and tangible magic.

I am so rich with my rituals
As I pour tea from Anja's teapot
And I stir porridge
To my health and good fortune
And I smile to hear
The steamy strains of the boiler
As it puffs up to pamper me with a bath.

Oh already the sun is in hiding
Risen into a pink blanket of cloud
Elusive now as embryo flesh
Oh where are you going? I ask.

And then it dawns on me!

Perhaps I am the only soul
In the whole town
To have glimpsed the sun
As it rose this morning.

Perhaps this means I am blessed for the day.

1994 – Totnes, Devon, UK

Queen Susan

Reddened hair clashes
Blood egg eyes
Susan,
Your flaming power
Yawns awakening.

When I see you
I see troubled beauty
Pesky charcoal clouds that drum
With thwarted rage.

Face painted clown
You tumble for the sake of humour
But I saw the silver dagger glint
In your eye
(You are a rebel. My friend.)

Susan.

Lift your defiance
Like a lead anchor
And throw it at your worst enemies
Shriek your spearheaded maori tongue
As they grip slime
Refuse to hold them.

Your heart is a pounding muscle
And things that restrain can easily be
Discarded.

1994 – Boulder, Colorado, US

Over You

I am sorry to say
That you leech from me
Your faint, dog-like excitement
When I stride past
And your fat lip
When I tell you
It. Is. Time. For. Me. To. Sleep.

There's something about you
That makes me think of lard
Congealed
Or the desperate buzz
Of breeding bacteria.

As you will not rest
Until you have dug into
All my sacred spaces
And left your scent
Mapped territory.

It is not even passion
And passion is easy.

You want to open me
Like a cheap market perfume and
Inhale your fill
Until you gag and crave plain air.

I must laugh.

Because you never see me.
You see everything you
Hope a woman could be
Should be.

You see the split second
Eternal
Meeting of desire
The spark

At the end of the
Far-reaching
Arc
And you expect
To capture that feeling
Like a biological specimen
In a pickle jar.

But I will never open up that far.

Because the love that
Beats through my heart
Belongs to me
And the honey, the nectar
That lives behind my nipples
Will only ever know
The salt of my flesh
No matter how hard you suck.

1994 – Boulder, Colorado, US

Apocalypse

There are many truths
Some are black and empty
Some radiate mushroom light.
But the underlying truth is loss.

So mother nature told me
When she showed me I must die
That no light or good or rainbow
Can divert
The black destruction
Mouth of dirt.

Like the last sound I hear
Could be the cracking of my own ribs
Or the splintering of glass and metal
Or the screams of thousands of smoke-filled lungs.

As the death the dark
That we all deny
Is not like this pretty
Wyoming sky
It blisters beauty and
It crushes bone.

Death will wipe the floor with you.
She will bring all her gore for you.
Until nothing becomes nothing
Becomes nothing becomes
Nothing.

1994 – Boulder, Colorado, US

Neurosis

Reaching for the
Cheap colour
Cocktail
She drinks the
Self-disgust
Of a
Short-lived
Sugar-pleasure
Fills her
Head
With neon
Til it
Circles
The carousel
Of its own
Sickly delights
And the world
Is once
Again
Candyfloss
Or feigns to be.

1995 – Totnes, Devon, UK

Harney's Peak

My vision roams the land in silence
See clouds pass softly unfolding sequels
Their nonchalant respect to the mortal efforts
Of me, their friend, and momentary equal.

Granite and crystals sparkle majestic
This pointed peak this summit arrival
With thinning breath and steep heart testing
And breath that pounds to the edge of survival.

Below me rocks still huddle snugly
In forested hills as black as jet
Like the hush of an animal subtle, unspoken
The movement of the sky in shadows reflect.

Lonely as the top winds point precisely
Shivering to be naked with the taste of fear
Like the brave who opens her furs and protection
To the final rest, exquisitely near.

1994 - The Black Hills, South Dakota, US

Holy Desire

Desire is everywhere

The tree desires the sun
In it's reach
The magpie desires
The glint of gold
In it's beak
Earth desires the rain
Wind desires the clouds
Breath desires the
Milk of Goddesses
Fat and happy
Against the breath
Even the child desires,
Reminds us that laughter
Desires our bellies that
Laughter wants it's wicked
Way with us.

Bodies desire desire.
Navigate us together like
Magnets or polar points
Like a compass seeking poise
And stillness at the centre
Of the storm of all this
Wanting it wanting it wanting it
Fighting it fighting it fighting it.

Desire is a simple thing
When felt
When sensed
When allowed to move.

Desire is the voice of God
The outbreath in the frost
The giggle in the stars
Not the bane of our existence
Not the keeper of some
Twisted human prison
That we must punish ourselves
To sit inside
Bereft and flagellating

Remember this remember this:

Desire is the tree towards the sun
The birds towards the flock
The rock towards erosion
And the bones towards decay.

Desire is the heartache of
Our ancestors who would
Have given it all ten times over
Just to have known us
For a moment.

It's the feathered
Path in the mist
It's the cackle
Of the hag from the ashes
Who should carry revenge
In her burned and charcoal heart
But delivers instead a gift
Like a whisper in our dreaming
Like a shadow or a light
In the woods
Whose call we have plainly
Failed to understand.

Because even the smell of it
Can break a fragile person
In two
Can draw daggers on the school gate
Can turn mothers to kill
Their daughters dead
Like all is well
Like it was all meant to be that way.

Instead of this way…
Instead of the song of one human
Into the ear of another
Instead of touch in the darkness
From one woman to a brother
Instead of the warmth of galaxies
Or the pull of oceans
As they surrender to the tide
In the exact same way
My sex surrenders to
The pull of a holy man
As he begs me
To speak again of the old ways
As he begs me to
Speak it into the ears of babes
As he begs me
To speak it to speak it just to speak it.

Desire is the witch's song
Desire is the holy prayer
Is all.
Bring our bodies
Back to power
And let everything else
Let the empires of thought
Let the fleets of war
Fall.

2018 – Kings Cross, London, UK

Queen of the Witches

My mother
My middle name
Goddess of the hunt
Driven by the fierce
Derived from dog nature
Courted by fire and
Dancing holy deer
Fucked by the wild
Ruled by the moon
Bringer of fertile power
The one whose face you can
Scream in as you birth
The one who sings
Against a drumbeat
And the oldest form of love on earth
Summoning the women
To her side
Guarding the babes
From the nettles
Dreaming deep in the
Woodland with all it's
Black secrets
Running barefoot
Into bracken where the
Truth is always found:

Diana
Huntress of the stars
Queen of the Witches
Call her name.

2013 – St Paul's, London, UK

Victimhood

Should a vampire's
Tender fangs softly
Drill the willing
Peach of my neck
I would touch the
Flawless satin
Of his evil and
Draw him closer in.

Even as he sucks me
Under cover of velvet
Would I lean my
Dropping head
Brush away the
Mist of hair and
Kiss the scarlet charries
That he feeds me
So succinct between
My lips.

1994 - Totnes, Devon, UK

Feminine Rising

Daddy Daddy
You bastard
I'm through.

But not quite
Don't you know it
I'm still
Talking to you.

I say
Alone
Daddy
Alone Alone
On your
Throne.

Where you order
You control
With your will
You say
Never ever
No I'm never
Gonna feel.

And my mother
Daddy
She heard your
Commands and
She let you.

She heard your
Commands and
She let you.

And so I withdrew like
An enemy
Daddy
Behind enemy lines
And I threw
Daddy
Bombs over your
Garden fence
Bombs through your
Letterbox
Until one day
I heard you
We'd both been
Weakened
By the battalions
Of our defence

And you said
Woman.

And you said
Woman.

And you said
Woman
Believe me
I'm a dancer
Not a slave-driver

And I said
Man
I know it
And I am
The Dance.

1995 - Totnes, Devon, UK

The Wolf

The wolf is
Not at the door
To harm you…

But to beckon you
To come…

To invite you
To follow…

To turn your
Attention to the
Silence and to
Starlight…

To pad with him
Softly and to
Trust his call…

Deeper and colder
Into the mountain
You go…

To the place where
You are food
To the frost.

And you know.

2022 - Bern, Switzerland

Jam-Making

The sky is streaked and
Surrendering
Like clear water
Clouding with ink.

So the crescent moon
Winks its silver sickle
Turns the other cheek and
Grins with ancient knowing.

Still in the thin distance…..
The night sky echoes
With the shriek of ravens
And pale, moonlight branches
Chilled to the bone are
Shivering like tin.

But not me.
The sinner.
As I pour the berries in.

1994 - Washbourne, Devon UK

Belief System

A man would believe
Until his flesh is falling from his body
Until he feels the breath
Tighten and take hold
A man would believe
In the rescue
In the saints coming
In the doctors
In it all
A man would believe.

I know a man who is rotting
From the inside
His flesh is falling.

No known cause.
No disease even
To pin his hopes on.

5 injections in.

2022 - Bern, Switzerland

Witches Love Dandelions

Eins, zwei, drei, fier
Dandelions are growing here
Funf, sechs, seiben, acht
Dandelions are magick fact
Neun, Sehn, Elf und Zwölf
Dandelion for strength and health
Dreizehn brave and dreizhen true
Puff! The spell is gone from you.

2022 - Selital, Switzerland

Spirit

I am a woman with
Deep spirit
And I see
Lots of you out there with
Deep spirit
Who know that
Peace on earth
Starts it's embryonic growth
In the beating cells of
Our own bloody hearts
And this knowledge
Is as fierce as
The phoenix who
Calls for the
Ends of the earth
And let me tell you
You don't
Get more powerful than that
And so
Deny it if you must
Tinker with your victimhood
In the junkyard
Of your rusted dreams
But know that
Deep down there
On the axis where the tide changes
And shifts the whole movement of seas
Is the possibility to
Change your life
Anytime you please
The possibility to
Change your world
Anytime you please
Is possibility.

1993 - Totnes, Devon UK

Artio

Loneliness hits
The certainty
That all else is
That nothing is
And everything is
Forsaken
Gone already to dust
Too late too soon.

Elsewhere.

The festivities ring
Holy ancient she is
Battleworn
Settled in her cave
Like the mother bear
Before winter
Ready to shut in
Called downwards
Not for riches
But for rest.

For she will rise again.
For she will strike.
For she will eat the damned.

And not because of
All this human counsel
Not because of these
Wisdom-keepers
Who keep on
Vying for her influence.

Borne instead from the jagged
Risen from cut-throat ice
Out of celestial silence
And the terror
That lives in the children now.

Mother bear
It is necessary
Mother bear
That the old Gods
Mother bear
Breathe again.

2022 - Bärenplatz, Bern, Switzerland

Lullaby for a Miscarriage

There are rhythms inside me
Silent as the sleeping moon
Simple the lullaby as it croons
So you cannot see me
Does that mean you disbelieve?
Existence is as fleeting
As the clouds crossing the eyes
Of this parting child singing
Mummy you will lose me
I do not belong
Drifting off
Letting go
Drifting off
All along.

2017 - Totnes, Devon UK

Over-Eating

Bother my bigness
I want to fly
Not be bound
By bulbous
Blubber and
Bones as heavy
As a horse.

(I stuff down baby bananas
To feed my brooding remorse
And silence my resentment on sweetness
Until it surfaces for second course.)

1995 - Totnes, Devon UK

Happy Families

It is my turn I hope
You will hear what I say
For centuries
We all know
It has been this way
From the beginning
Let us start at mine
Violence and fear
Threats that curled my behaviour
I bowed like a vine to the sun of
My father
(I followed my Mother's example
And together we schemed
To keep his pathway clear)

Still. In spite of all our efforts…
Every once in a while…

All that repressed rage
Another day at the office my dear
Would come bursting
Out of his jugular
And my mother would get
Blown to the floor
Under the tidal wave of his temper
And I would get
Pushed underground
Beneath the pestle and mortar
Of her hatred
And then…

Well I only had the kittens to torment
Until my brother came along
And you can imagine what I did to him.

So onward we rolled
One big happy family
And onward I tumbled
Into girlhood and a gradual
Evolution from
Tops of the Pops to
Just Seventeen
Bombarded my mind with
Images of women
So complete and squeaky clean
They gave me clips and bits
And tips on my tits
Oh you won't get a boyfriend
'Til you stop those spreading hips..

One thousand and ten
Ways to please your men
And I was thrilled!
I embarked upon a voyage
Based on paradox
As so happy was I to attract you,
That I popped a pill of osetrogen
Gladly and figured
If you wanted to fuck me
Oh if you would only desire me!
Then whole crowds would cheer me
Like I'd scored
Another point on the path I was
To getting myself a man
Yes I almost submitted to the
Corporate Master Plan.

Until…

I went and got myself a
Place at college
And my poor mother
How she cried
I thought you were going to be an XYZ,
And then my Father joined in:
Theatre and English?
You'll never get a job!
And to this day he was right
Oh Thank God
That in spite of my education
My upbringing my culture
My gruelling preparation for
A suitable vocation
Still something somewhere
Inside of me won.

And I began to ask questions..

And I looked at my Father
And I said

Why?

And gradually my skip turned
Into a dance
And I laughed and I yelled
Like pink champagned I spat and I spewed
Why why why why why why why?

(Oh I followed orders still
For I was trained to read the danger signs
White Knuckles Black Brow)

But I went on singing sarcasm under my breath…

'Til my mother saw me
And blamed her distress
On my beatnik ways
How she held my brother tight
And they pined
For the remembrance of
Better days..
'Til my Father leaned over me
Where are you going?

And I replied:
Nowhere!
Nowhere –
I lied…

But it sparkled through my pupils
The part I had to hide.

And then I fell in love
And that's when I realised
That it wasn't just anger
That most of it was pain
Yes I think we've all been there
We've all reached out in vain
We've screamed out our hunger
And scratched oneanother's flesh bare
In the naked search
For our own missing link
Until we realised
Every one of us
That there was actually nothing there…

And that's when I cupped him
Like a stranger in my hands
Watched him wistful fall away
Float like an autumn leaf downstream

And I was left banging the drum of my tantrum
Tearing down the walls of churches
I was left searching for the blood
Of my religion
Only to hear the solemn bell toll
To silence my appeal:

Alone. Alone. Alone.

1996 - Totnes, Devon UK

Grandmother

Line worn
Grave drawn
Bear it child
Life is long.

Duty bound
House ground
Black scarf
Left til last.

Peasant strife
Such is life
Bear it child
Life is long.

1995 - Totnes, Devon UK

City Walk

Side stepping on the pavement
High on fumes and
Good coffee and the
Pace of it.

The dance and
This constant weaving
There's a grace to it.

See the man who
Bikes to conquer…

And the women in their heels who
Try not to falter…

And that young man who's running
Like none of this is
Fast enough?

Or the black woman in the
Tight tan leather
Who looks so good I break out
Grinning…

To the mother who pulls
Her schoolboy onwards
Like even he should be winning

And it's the hate in it…

Black man striding
Headphones on
And I wonder if it's hip hop
Or whether I'm a racist?

Or the woman who
Believes she is
Way ahead of the game Sista
Waaay ahead of the likes of me
And it makes me want to slap her
Cold and dark and whisper
Urgent with my age:
Listen to me, Lady
Listen…
And I will tell you this for free –
That you too will travel
Through life
Searching for shamans
But finding only
Doctors.

Oh there's a pace to it
A sheer relentless
Grace to it.

Muslim walking
Headphones on
And I wonder if she's a
Terrorist
Or whether I'm a racist?
And the pregnant woman
Slowing against the grain
Like a huge ship swaying and
Cradling her belly
Trying already in vain
To protect it from all this
Violence.

See it's the pace of it
The speed of it
Right past the dragons
Into the heart of it.

Posh boy
Pink tie pale suit
Cigarette dangling
Because he was born for this
You see
All this shit
Belongs
To him.

Or the hot guy in the hoodie
With the shaved head and the eye-contact
Saying yes
Hoodie
Yes
Hoodie
You could take me in an instant
Hoodie
In a heartbeat I'd be yours
Because I only
Ever really loved
Two smells
Believe me
Hoodie
Only two that
Ever really got me in the end…

The skin of my beloveds
Or the sharp hit
Of the metal of
This City's river
As I turn the corner
And I find her:

Raging in the sunlight.
Every. Single. Time.

2015 - Islington to the Southbank, London UK

Cunt

This ain't no
Peepshow Sunshine
This is yearning power
Huge and generating
As the chasm of a wave.

1996 - Totnes, Devon UK

Swimming in the Aare

Ice to liquid
It's a holy descent
Full of melt and snow
Full of the bright
Delivering turquoise to the salty
From the summits
I am a child in her speed
I am wrestling in her flow
Trying to punch for glory
When she has me
Like the hawk
Who watches from the banks
Ready for the
Snake in the grass and
My whole body is
Given to this velocity
To the absolute mineral bite of her
Rapidity and precision.

Like the darkness giving way to the light
I succumb.
Like the darkness giving way to the light
I'm undone.

2022 - Bern, Switzerland

Gantrisch Bilberries

The sun weakens
A tiny chill gathers up courage
And turns to face
The coming clouds
As the mountain women
Tell me that it's
Cranberry season now,
That the bilberries are gone
Both to birdseed and
Zum nächsten Jahr.

Oh the land and the strength
That pounds from them
Their boots as sturdy as
The mountain backdrop
And the millenia those peaks have
Stood their ground.

Same as it ever was.

Women who know the ways of the place.
Who know the heartbeat
Of these heights
Who have whiskers to
Listen for the winds and
Eyelashes to sense
The coming of the snow.

I came here looking
For sustenance and for soul.

But the berries are crumpled
And I have missed their
Bilberry song.

Brief as it was.
But strong.

Loud as a clarion call
Competing with the cowbells
Still the bilberries held their fleeting
Chorus to the heavens
Still they gave their all.

Some things don't belong to you.
Some things are crying out for you
If only you would notice.

Don't forget them
In your fortitude
In your struggle
In your myriad insistences
All the intricacies of your reasoning
Don't forget them.

They are lameting your distraction
Even now
As they call out
Hard as winter's slap
To awaken you to know:

The whole world will
Open up it's magic
If you would only
Bless it first
With the breath
Of your attention.

Sit a while.

2022 - Selital, Switzerland

Mother

It seems we are both scarred
Out battle wounds cut
Bloodless to brittle bones
Their chinking sounds as hollow as
Porcelain versus glass
Still my body is not empty
But is brimming with
Hurt and hate and love
And the remembrance of
Wishes that whispered
From my tiny chest –
That you suck me clean of this
Festering disease
And we rest, tired and worn
But bleeding together.

Instead, I was born of your hurts
And through me you reaped
The Universe of yours.

1994 - Totnes, Devon UK

Land of Kings

What will I be?
What channel will tumble
Open

What miracles
Previously
Unspoken

Might come
Into focus like
The slow turning
Of a lens

Like the torpid
Waking from a
Dream

Into clarity
Pristine as an
Alpine stream

What luck
What bounty
What a Kingdom.

2022 - Bern, Switzerland

Julia Lally is a wife, mother, mentor, musician and playwright. Author of productions *The Misdemeanors of the House of Ravenous* and *Hunchback of Bethnal Green.* Composer of album *Spirit.*

Artio is her first published book of poetry.

You can find out more at www.julialally.com/artio
Or follow her on IG: @thejulialally